DEC   2006

04440 4953

CH

How to Draw
Cartoons

This book is dedicated to Jasmine.

Published in the United States of America by The Child's World®
PO Box 326 • Chanhassen, MN 55317-0326
800-599-READ • www.childsworld.com

Acknowledgments
Design and Production: The Creative Spark, San Juan Capistrano, CA
Series Editor: Elizabeth Sirimarco Budd
Illustration: Rob Court

Library of Congress Cataloging-in-Publication Data
Court, Rob, 1956–
  How to draw cartoons / by Rob Court.
    p. cm. — (The Scribbles Institute)
  ISBN 1-59296-149-5 (library bound : alk. paper)
  1. Cartooning—Technique—Juvenile literature. I. Title.
  NC1320.C63 2004
  741.5—dc22
                                        2004003730

How to Draw
Cartoons

Rob Court

The Child's World®

It is not enough to believe what you see,
you must also understand what you see.

—Leonardo da Vinci

Parents and Teachers,

Children love to draw! It is an essential part of a child's learning process. Drawing skills are used to investigate both natural and constructed environments, record observations, solve problems, and express ideas. The purpose of this book is to help students advance through the challenges of drawing and to encourage the use of drawing in school projects. The reader is also introduced to the elements of visual art—lines, shapes, patterns, form, texture, light, space, and color—and their importance in the fundamentals of drawing.

The Scribbles Institute is devoted to educational materials that keep creativity in our schools and in our children's dreams. Our mission is to empower young creative thinkers with knowledge in visual art while helping to improve their drawing skills. Students, parents, and teachers are invited to visit our Web site—www.scribblesinstitute.com—for useful information and guidance. You can even get advice from a drawing coach!

Contents

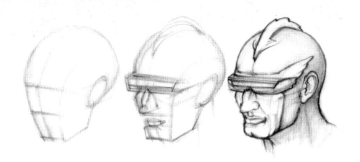

Drawing Cartoons Is Fun!

As a cartoonist, you can sketch shapes and lines that come to life on paper. You can create a comic strip that tells funny jokes, or a comic book about a superhero. You can even create characters for an animated film.

The easy steps in this book will help you draw cartoons for school projects or for fun. Find a big piece of paper and a pencil. You can get started right now!

Telling a Story
A cartoon is a picture that tells a story. You can draw action lines that show the movements of a bird. Or you can add words to create a conversation between a dog and cat.

Choosing Your Own Style

As you develop cartoon characters, you can experiment with different drawing styles. You can use a style that exaggerates a character's features, such as huge eyes and a tiny nose. Simple, bold lines can express characters' emotions. Realistic drawing uses details from real life. With practice, you'll develop your own drawing style.

Drawing with Shapes

Drawing a cartoon character is easy when you start with basic shapes. Use shapes to show the features of a man's face. Sketch these shapes lightly in case you want to erase them later.

1   Start by drawing an oval for the man's head. A smaller oval and two circles make the eyes and nose.

2   Draw two triangles for his hair and two ovals for his ears. Add a shape for his mouth and two lines for his neck.

3   Now draw darker lines to show his features. Notice the details of his ears, teeth, and hair.

1   An oval creates a woman's face. Sketch two half circles for her eyes and a diamond for her mouth. Add two ovals for ears.

2   Next, sketch the shapes for her hair. Draw curved lines for her eyes and nose. Add two lines for her neck. Do you like the shapes you've drawn?

3   Trace a darker line around the shape of her face. Pay attention to the **outlines** of her ears and hair. Add details such as earrings, lips, eyelashes, and eyebrows.

8

Drawing with Lines

Drawing an outline around the edge of the shapes you've made forms a punk rocker's face. Keep drawing until you like the outline.

Punk Rocker

round corners form the face

1 A rectangle is the basic shape for this mean-looking guy. Draw rectangles for his head, chin, and pug nose.

2 Next, sketch the shapes for his eye, nose, and ear. Sketch the outline around the edges of his face. Add curved and pointy lines for his hair.

3 Now draw darker lines to show his features. Notice the details of his ears, teeth, and hair.

HOT TIP

Expressions

By placing simple lines and dots in an oval, you can show emotions and facial expressions. Try sketching several ovals on a piece of paper. Think of an emotion, then draw dots and lines to express it. Use the examples at left to get you started.

Character Development

Creating a character for a comic book or animated movie is called character development.

Try experimenting with ovals, circles, and triangles to develop your character's personality.

Shaping the Face

A person's face shows personality and expresses emotions. Start sketching your character's face by combining different shapes. You can change facial characteristics by altering positions and combinations of shapes. Keep sketching until you like the face you've drawn.

Features

Once you have drawn the shape of the face, you can experiment with facial features. By changing features, you can change the personality and appearance of your character.

Costumes and Props

Costumes and props, such as a hat and tie, can tell viewers something about your character. A student carries a pencil and book. An elf wears a tall, pointed hat.

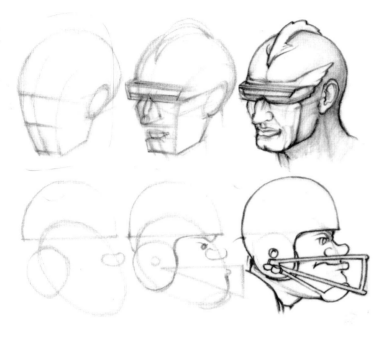

Proportions

You can draw curved guidelines to divide the **proportions** of a superhero's face. This will help you place the facial features in a realistic way.

The proportions of this football player's head are exaggerated. A small helmet and large chin show that he is big and strong. Notice how his eyebrow and bottom lip express his tough personality.

Body Language

Body language is the way people's body and their facial expressions describe their reaction to a situation. Use body language to illustrate a story without using words.

Hands on hips and a tapping foot show an impatient grandma.

Large, drooping eyes, a flower, and a hand behind the back illustrates a boy who is apologizing.

Spread fingers and action lines show a frightened man and mouse.

Feet off the ground show a startled reaction.

11

Sketching basic shapes helps you create the proportions of your character's body. Triangles form the body of a tall, slender girl.

Construction Worker

1. Sketch a circle for the head and two triangle shapes for the body. Ovals make the worker's nose and feet.

2. Sketch the shapes for his helmet, hand, and tool box. Draw ovals for his eyes and ears. Sketch lines for his shirt.

3. Draw darker outlines for his helmet, head, and body. Include details such as his eyes, shirt sleeve, suspenders, and tools.

1. Sketch a circle and an oval for the body and head. Add an arched shape for his legs.

2. Add shapes for his hands and feet. Sketch outlines to form his body. Add details such as a ponytail and eyebrows.

3. Draw final outlines to show the roundness of his body.

![HOT TIP] Guidelines

Cartoonists use guidelines when sketching superhero action figures. These lines create a framework for the character's body and costume.

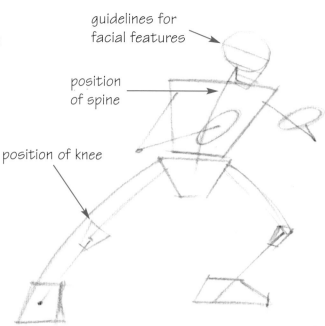

guidelines for facial features

position of spine

position of knee

Action Figure

1 This superhero's body is ready to fight. Sketch guidelines to show the position of his body. Start by sketching the shape for his head, chest, hands, and the lower half of his body. Sketch the guidelines for his legs. Add the shapes for his feet.

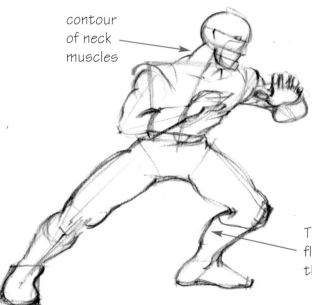

contour of neck muscles

2 The outlines that form his powerful arms, legs, and chest are called **contour** lines. Sketch curved and angled lines until other features, such as his hands and feet, are formed. Carefully follow the guidelines to draw his face.

This contour line shows a flexed muscle prepared to thrust forward.

3 Do you like the position of his arms and legs? Do the curves of his muscles look natural? Continue by drawing the final, darker outlines that form his body. Concentrate on details such as his mask, gloves, and shoes. His facial expression shows confidence and determination.

Drawing Animals

Cartoon animals are fun to draw. By sketching basic shapes, you can develop the character of a happy dog.

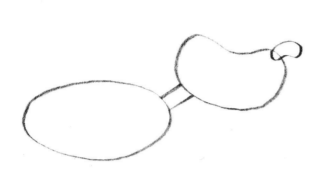

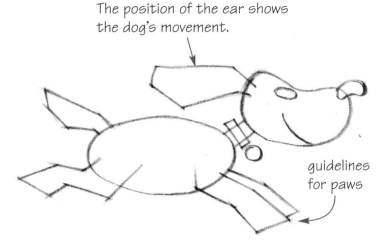

The position of the ear shows the dog's movement.

guidelines for paws

Happy Dog

1 Start by drawing an oval for the dog's body. A kidney shape makes the head. A smaller kidney shape makes the nose. Add two lines for the neck.

2 Carefully sketch guidelines for the legs, ears, tail, and smile. Draw an oval for the eye and shapes for the collar.

Sketch short lines for fur.

shadow

3 Begin sketching the outlines to form the dog's body. To make a friendly expression, draw curved lines for a smile and eyebrows. Add the shape for the tongue.

4 Do you like what you've drawn? Finish by drawing darker outlines that form your happy cartoon dog. Add details such as dots for whiskers, spots on the fur, and a dark **tone** for the nose and collar.

Baseball Cat

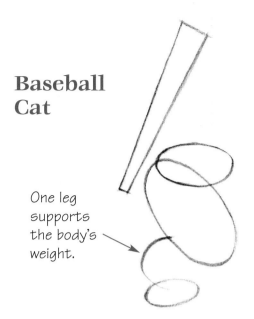

One leg supports the body's weight.

1. You can draw animals doing things only humans do in real life. Start by sketching ovals for the cat's head and body. Draw the shape for the baseball bat.

2. Next, draw the shapes for paws, which are holding the bat. Begin drawing the shapes for the eyes, ears, and nose. Sketch curved lines for the tail and legs.

knuckles and thumb

Showing the bottom of the paw exaggerates the action of stepping into the swing.

3. If you like the shapes you've drawn, begin sketching the outlines that form the cat's body. Draw the cat's fur, whiskers, and mouth.

action lines

eye on the ball

straight lines show a fastball

4. Finish your picture by drawing darker outlines for the cat's body. Finish drawing props such as the bat, jersey, and cap. Add stripes for the pattern on the cat's fur.

15

Patterns

You can create patterns by repeating lines or shapes.

Smart Turtle

1 Draw a shape for the turtle's shell. Make an oval for his head.

2 Draw shapes for his legs and tail and an oval for reading glasses. Sketch the book.

3 After drawing the outlines of the turtle, add patterns for his shell and toenails.

wood grain pattern

A pattern can illustrate a grassy area. How does the grass pattern change in the distance? **Vertical** lines make a fence in the background. Don't forget to draw a pattern on the cow.

A pattern of rectangles makes a brick wall. You can draw a person hiding behind it. Criss-crossing lines make a pattern on a man's suit and a dog's sweater. How can you tell the man is whistling?

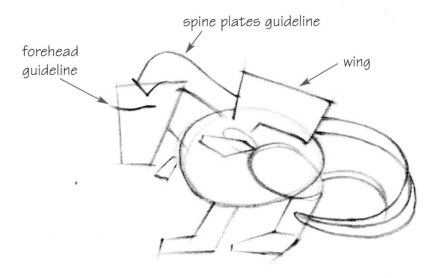

spine plates guideline

forehead
guideline

wing

Scaly Dragon

1 Sketch a large oval for the dragon's body and a smaller oval for the strong back leg. Make the shape for the dragon's head and a guideline for the neck.

2 Next, begin sketching guidelines for the neck, wings, legs, and claws. Take time to sketch the curves for its thick tail. Lightly sketch the guidelines for the spine plates.

HOT TIP **Natural Tails**

Instead of using angled lines, sketch curved lines to make the dragon's tail. Look for round parts of your dragon's body as you draw.

angled line   curved line

3 Continue by sketching outlines to form the dragon's body and tail. Carefully draw details of the head. Notice the contour lines that form the powerful claws. Add curved lines for the edge of the spine plates.

4 After drawing the final outlines, add patterns to make your dragon look real. Draw the pattern for its scaly skin only in a few areas. Patterns make the texture of its spine, belly, and wings.

Texture

How the surface of something feels is called texture. The texture of hair is different from the texture of trees and rocks. You can draw lines and patterns to create textures.

A pattern of short lines creates the prickly texture of a cactus or the beard on an old man's face. Lines and dots create the texture of a tree and a rock. The contour lines of an oversized chair make it look soft. The contour lines on the edge of the girl's bowl make it look smooth.

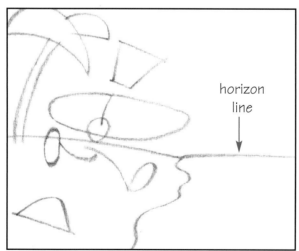

Surfer on the Beach

1 Draw the **horizon line.** Next, sketch ovals for the surfer's head, surfboard, and feet. Sketch guidelines for the surfer's arms and legs and for the palm tree.

2 Draw outlines to form the surfer's body and the landscape. Notice how lines and dots are used to create textures. How does the surface of the ocean change when it is closer to shore?

18

Imagine how these textures feel to the touch. Add these textures to the cartoon characters you draw.

reflection

smooth bone

curly fur

hard, bumpy surface

fluffy fur

pointy porcupine quills

short, bristly hair

feathers

HOT TIP **Less Detail**

When drawing hair, cartoonists usually leave out a lot of details. It takes less time if you don't draw every hair. Include strands to show the form, texture, or movement of the hair. By adding more strands in certain areas, you can create shading.

Hair

Hair can be bristly, curly, or smooth. The way you draw hair can illustrate a funny situation or a character's personality.

Three-Dimensional Form

With practice, you can change flat shapes into three-dimensional or "3-D" forms. Begin drawing a horse by making two ovals.

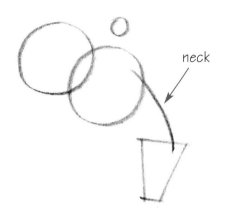

neck

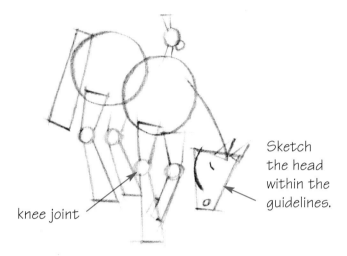

Sketch the head within the guidelines.

knee joint

Horse and Bird

1 Draw guidelines for the neck and head. Two circles form the body of the horse. Add a small circle for the body of the bird.

2 Sketch guidelines for the tail and legs. Draw circles for the leg joints. Begin sketching lines for the face and ears. A triangle forms the bird's tail.

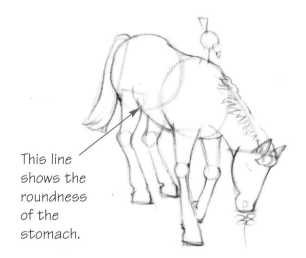

This line shows the roundness of the stomach.

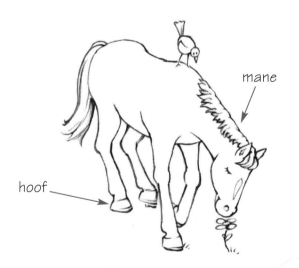

mane

hoof

3 Begin sketching the outlines for the horse, bird, and flower. Sketch lightly so you can make corrections. Curved lines show the roundness of the horse's body.

4 If you like what you've drawn, continue by carefully drawing the darker outlines of the horse's body. Include details for the mane and hooves.

20

Animation artists sketch different views of a character to determine how it will look in various positions. How does the form of a bird change as its body is rotated?

Flying Robot

1 By sketching two boxes, you can create the form of a robot. To make the boxes, you can use **perspective** drawing. Start by sketching guidelines that are angled to a **vanishing point.** Next, carefully draw the outlines of the boxes.

perspective guidelines

vanishing point •

2 Continue by sketching rectangles and boxes. Cartoonists call this "boxing-in" the shapes. Include the chest area, shoulders, face, and legs. Don't forget the jetpack to help this robot soar into space.

jet pack

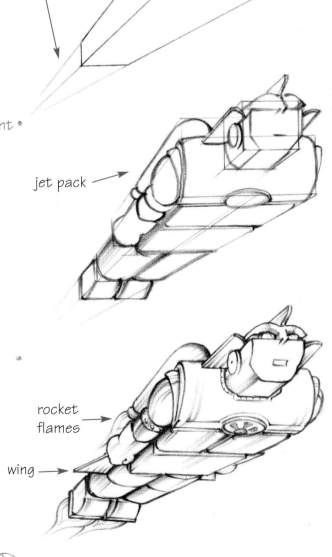

3 Does the robot seem to be getting larger as it flies toward you? Draw the final outlines for the arms, legs, feet, and stabilizing wings. By drawing Earth much smaller than the robot, it looks very far away.

rocket flames

wing

21

Light and Shadows

By using light and dark tones, you can create shadows. Drawing shadows helps you see a girl's form and the ground beneath her.

Girl and Butterfly

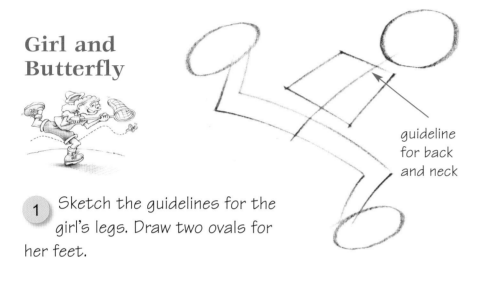

guideline for back and neck

1 Sketch the guidelines for the girl's legs. Draw two ovals for her feet.

Sketch curved lines to show roundness.

2 Draw the ovals for her hands, eyes, and ears. Now sketch the net. Draw guidelines for her legs. Press lightly with your pencil. This will make it easier to erase the shapes before drawing the shadows shown in step 4.

Light Source

Places where light comes from are called light sources. The sun is a light source. A lamp is also a light source. In the drawing below, a light source shines on a sphere. How do the shadows change as the light changes position?

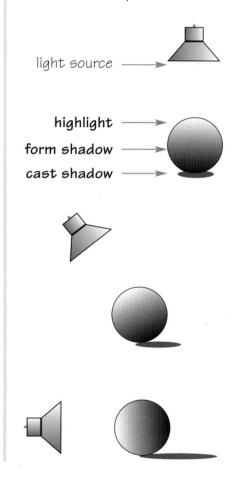

light source

highlight

form shadow

cast shadow

22

A falling hat shows the girl's movement toward the butterfly.

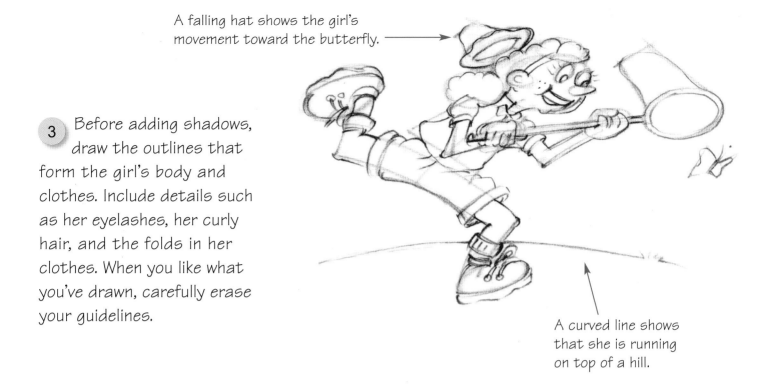

3 Before adding shadows, draw the outlines that form the girl's body and clothes. Include details such as her eyelashes, her curly hair, and the folds in her clothes. When you like what you've drawn, carefully erase your guidelines.

A curved line shows that she is running on top of a hill.

4 Start drawing shadows in areas where no light shines from the light source. Hold your pencil on its side, press firmly, and begin drawing the darkest shadows on the girl's body. Shadows will be lighter where more light shines. Lighten the pressure on your pencil as you draw lighter shadows. Fade the shadows away to the white of the paper where there are highlights. Remember to draw the cast shadow on the ground beneath her foot.

Contour lines show the net's pattern.

Don't forget the pattern on the butterfly's wings!

A dotted line shows motion.

cast shadow

23

Space and Composition

The white space of your paper can be transformed into a comic strip where cartoon characters live. The way you divide the space is called composition.

horizon line

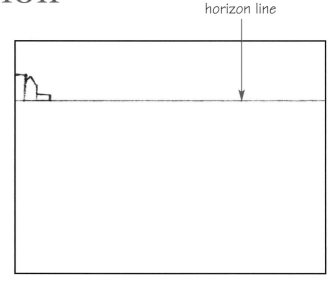

1. Draw straight lines for the borders of your comic strip panel. Next, draw the horizon line to the edges of the panel. Add shapes for buildings in the distance. The buildings are in the background.

background

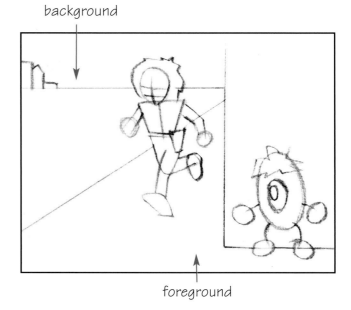

2. A rectangle creates the wall of a building where an alien creature can hide. The alien is in the foreground of the composition. Sketch the shapes for its body, eye, hands, and feet. Next, sketch the shapes for a boy in a running position. Add guidelines for his hair, gun, and boots. An angled line makes a sidewalk that disappears behind the building.

foreground

3. Draw the darker, final outlines that form the boy and the alien. Include details such as as fingers, hair, and action lines.

Dialogue

Cartoonists can tell a story with pictures and words. The comic strip panel below shows a conversation between a man and his daughter. Their dialogue is illustrated with word balloons. The man is speaking first, so his word balloon is at the top of the composition.

word balloon

What do the facial expressions and body language of the characters tell you? What do the props tell you?

You can only see part of the man's face. This makes him look closer to you. The girl is drawn smaller to make her look farther away.

Foreshortening

You have probably seen drawings in which an object or person looks as if it is coming toward you, popping out of the picture. The method used to achieve this is called foreshortening. Cartoonists use foreshortening to show what's most important in a picture. In the illustration below, what does the artist want you to see first?

Notice the foreshortening of the fingers and thumb as they come toward you.

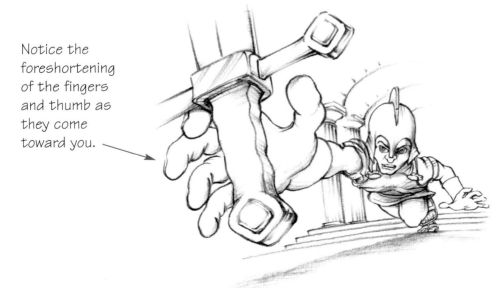

Compare the size of the sword and the warrior's right hand to his feet.

Ideas to Help You Tell a Story

Cartoonists can make a toaster sing a song about bread or use lettering for dramatic impact. These are examples of ways to make your story fun to read and easier to understand.

thought balloon

Animating objects, such as a toaster or a piece of bread, brings interesting characters to life. Shown above are two happy kitchen characters! The comic panel at right shows a girl thinking of a way to get some peace and quiet while watching TV. Notice the lines used to show the boy yelling.

Cat and Mouse

1 A cat is in the background, waiting for a mouse. The mouse gets ready to run for the hole. Facial expressions, body language, and composition set the stage for action.

2 A cloud of dust and speed lines show a quick takeoff. Dramatic foreshortening shows the movement of the cat's paw. Tiny beads of sweat show a frightened mouse. Bold lettering adds a loud sound effect.

Which Pencil Should You Use?

A standard "2B" or "2SOFT"' pencil works well for most drawings, but other pencils can make your drawing even more interesting.

Pencils are numbered according to how hard or soft the lead is. You'll find this number written on the pencil. A number combined with the letter "H" means the lead is hard (2H, 3H, 4H, etc.). When you draw with hard leads, the larger the number you use, the lighter and thinner your lines will be.

A number combined with the letter "B" means the lead is soft (2B, 4B, 6B, etc.). The lines you draw will get darker and thicker with larger numbers. Sometimes you will read "2SOFT" or "2B" on standard pencils used for schoolwork. When you see the letter "F" on a pencil, it means the pencil is of medium hardness.

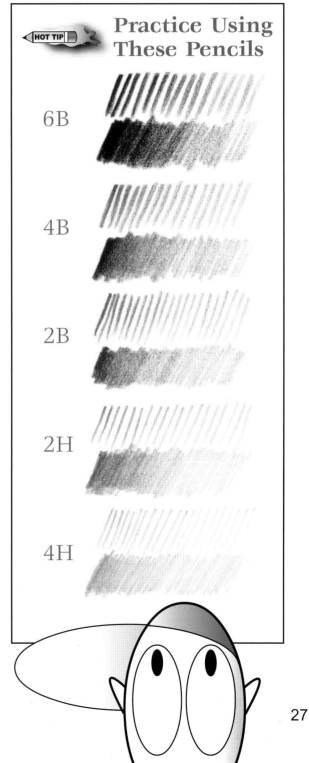

HOT TIP

Practice Using These Pencils

6B

4B

2B

2H

4H

27

Drawing with Color

By using colored pencils, you can make a drawing more exciting. Create the colors by mixing yellow, blue, red, and black.

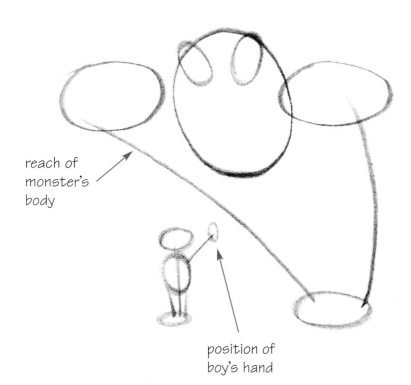

reach of monster's body

position of boy's hand

1 The monster's large hands and exaggerated shapes and the foreshortening of its body make this illustration dramatic. Sketch curved guidelines for the monster's long body. Ovals form its large hands, head, eyes, and feet.

Sketch a small oval for the boy's hand. It is the focus of the illustration. Continue by making ovals for his head, body, and feet. Notice the guidelines for his outstretched arm, neck, and legs.

2 Sketch the outlines of the monster's body. Draw the shapes for its ears, snout, nostrils, and large mouth. Next, draw shapes for the strong fingers and sharp claws. Sketch an oval for the monster's belly.

Sketch ovals for the boy's ears and nose. Draw the outlines of his hair, face, and neck. Next, sketch the outlines for the teddy bear held in his arm. Continue with outlines of his arms, legs, and feet.

guideline for spine plates

Broken lines show the texture of fur.

His face expresses confidence.

3 Carefully draw outlines for the monster's sharp teeth, claws, ears, bony spine plates, belly, tail, and toenails. The boy is in his pajamas. Do you think he is awake or only dreaming?

When you like the lines you've drawn, carefully erase all guidelines and prepare to add color.

Toenails on the ground tell us the monster has been stopped just before jumping.

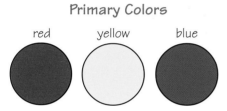

Primary Colors

red   yellow   blue

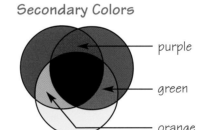

Secondary Colors

purple

green

orange

HOT TIP

Mixing primary colors creates secondary colors.

Adding one color on top of another is called layering. To learn how to layer primary colors, try using only yellow, blue, red, and black in this drawing.

4 Lightly shade the monster's fur with a yellow pencil. Apply more pressure to darken shadowy areas. Now lightly shade the boy's face and hands.

darker yellow

Tension lines show that the monster is struggling to stand on its toenails. Notice the lines showing the simple motion of the boy's hand.

Darker shadows begin to appear.

What color do you get when you mix blue with yellow?

Next, add blue to your drawing. Shade the monster's fur and belly with a light blue tone. Add a darker tone of blue in areas where there are more shadows. Add light blue to shade the teddy bear.

Mixing Colored Pencils Is Fun!

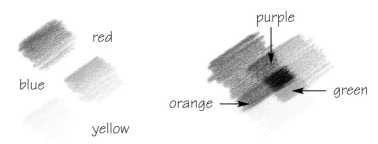

red

blue

yellow

purple

orange

green

Fun things start to happen when you add red to this illustration. Lightly shade the inside of the monster's mouth and spine plates with red. A darker red calls attention to the monster's tongue. Add a layer of light red on its face, hands, ears, and feet. Add light red to the boy's skin. What color do you get when you add red on top of yellow? Remember to make darker shadows that are farther away from the light source, such as the boy's pajamas. Shading with black creates 3-D forms. Highlights and shadows make realistic details such as hair and fur.

30

cast shadow

The Artist's Studio

Artists need a special place where they can relax and concentrate on their work.

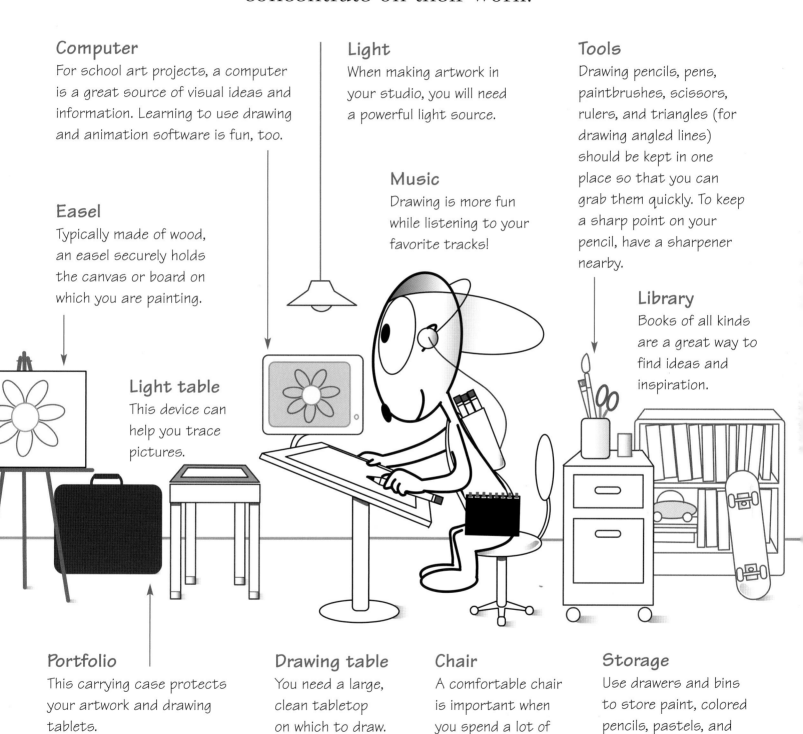

Computer
For school art projects, a computer is a great source of visual ideas and information. Learning to use drawing and animation software is fun, too.

Easel
Typically made of wood, an easel securely holds the canvas or board on which you are painting.

Light table
This device can help you trace pictures.

Portfolio
This carrying case protects your artwork and drawing tablets.

Light
When making artwork in your studio, you will need a powerful light source.

Music
Drawing is more fun while listening to your favorite tracks!

Drawing table
You need a large, clean tabletop on which to draw.

Chair
A comfortable chair is important when you spend a lot of time drawing.

Tools
Drawing pencils, pens, paintbrushes, scissors, rulers, and triangles (for drawing angled lines) should be kept in one place so that you can grab them quickly. To keep a sharp point on your pencil, have a sharpener nearby.

Library
Books of all kinds are a great way to find ideas and inspiration.

Storage
Use drawers and bins to store paint, colored pencils, pastels, and other supplies.

Glossary

A **cast shadow** is the shadow that a person, animal, or object throws on the ground, a wall, or other feature.

A **contour** is the outline of something; in your drawings, a contour line follows the natural shape of a cartoon character's features.

A **form shadow** is a shadow in a drawing that shows the form or shape of a person, animal, or object.

A **highlight** is the area (or areas) in a drawing that receives the most light from the light source.

The **horizon line** is the point at which the sky and the earth appear to meet.

An **outline** is a line that shows the shape of an object, animal, or person.

Perspective is the art of picturing objects on a flat surface, like a piece of paper, so that they appear to be in the distance.

Proportions are the relations between two or more things in terms of their size; if something is in proportion, all its parts are in proper relation to each other.

A **tone** is a lighter or darker shade of a color.

A **vanishing point** in a drawing is the point in the distance where two parallel lines meet.

A **vertical** line is drawn straight up and down; a person standing up is in a vertical position.

Index

About the Author

Rob Court is a designer and illustrator. He started the Scribbles Institute™ to help people learn about the importance of drawing and visual art.